THE

PENDLETON™

FIELD GUIDE TO

CAMPFIRE

COOKING

THE

PENDLETON™

FIELD GUIDE TO

CAMPFIRE

COOKING

PENDLETON WOOLEN MILLS

Recipes by Sarah Keats and Lindsey Bro

CHRONICLE BOOKS

SAN FRANCISCO

Copyright © 2022 Pendleton Woolen Mills, Inc.
Photographs used under license from Shutterstock.com.

Library of Congress Cataloging-in-Publication Data

Names: Keats, Sarah, author. | Bro, Lindsey, author. | Pendleton Woolen
Mills, Inc., organizer.
Title: The Pendleton field guide to campfire cooking / Pendleton Woolen
Mills ; recipes by Sarah Keats, Lindsey Bro.
Description: Series: The Pendleton field guide series
Identifiers: LCCN 2021036796 | ISBN 9781797207599 (hardcover)
Subjects: LCSH: Outdoor cooking. | LCGFT: Cookbooks.
Classification: LCC TX823 .P44 2022 | DDC 641.5/78--dc23
LC record available at https://lccn.loc.gov/2021036796

Manufactured in China.

Illustrations by Derek Nobbs.
Design by Kayla Ferriera.

Bragg is a registered trademark of Bragg Live Food Products, LLC; Broccolini
is a registered trademark of Mann Packing Co., Inc.; Halloumi is a registered
trademark of Ministry Of Energy, Commerce and Industry, Government
Agency, Cyprus; Jacobsen is a registered trademark of Jacobsen LLC;
Kerrygold Dubliner is a registered trademark of Ornua Co-Operative Limited
Company; Maldon is a registered trademark of Maldon Crystal Salt Company
Limited Limited Company; Microplane is a registered trademark of Grace
Manufacturing Inc.; Nutella is a registered trademark of Ferrero S.p.A.;
Rainier is a registered trademark of Pabst Brewing Company, LLC; San
Marzano is a registered trademark of San Marzano Vini S.p.A.; Tillamook
is a registered trademark of Tillamook County Creamery Association.

10 9 8 7 6 5 4 3

Chronicle books and gifts are available at special quantity discounts to
corporations, professional associations, literacy programs, and other
organizations. For details and discount information, please contact our
premiums department at corporatesales@chroniclebooks.com or at
1-800-759-0190.

Chronicle Books LLC
680 Second Street
San Francisco, California 94107
www.chroniclebooks.com

CONTENTS

THE SHORE

THE DESERT

CONNECTING AROUND THE CAMPFIRE

The best thing about campfire cooking is the connections we make. Gathered around a fire with friends and family, set in nature's landscapes, we tap into the great outdoors with all five senses. These opportunities remind us to be present and appreciate the land for all it offers.

Presence is a lifelong study with many teachers, made evident by breathtaking scenery, fresh air, clear water, and a wild abundance of flora and fauna. Camping is an exercise in finding balance: These connections to our world and our campmates offer us a break from everyday stressors and annoyances, bringing us back into the moment and offering peace in our existence without all the extra *stuff*. Connecting with presence out there—soaking up the visuals, the scents, the sounds—helps us find peace when we're *not* out there.

For us, presence is both the process and the goal of camping: It is almost impossible to camp without some constant acknowledgment of the moment. From the detailed preparation of the trip to setting up camp just right to planning and preparing meals, the rituals and rhythms of camping connect us to the present, giving us ample opportunities to create the moments we take with us as memories when we pack out again.

Camping is elemental, peeling away the layers of modern living to help us enjoy the simplest of practices for exactly what they are. In it, we exercise our need for freedom, taking ourselves outside of cities, schedules, and screens. Out there, the only real schedule we're bound to is the sun's path across the sky. Our to-do lists contain only camp chores, recreation, leisure, meals, and snacks. With little pressure to do anything other than be present, we're able to sit around the campfire—wrapped in warm wool blankets—mesmerized by a chorus of smoke, crackles, and sparks. We keenly equip ourselves with necessities and practical comforts, balancing our wants and needs within our cargo space. We make any campsite our home

for the time being. We sleep deeply and rise early. We run, play, hike, swim, labor, and rest. And, boy, do we eat. We cook as much to entertain ourselves as to fill our bellies and warm our hearts.

The Pendleton Field Guide to Campfire Cooking aims to connect us to the great outdoors through food. Using the senses as much as the ingredients themselves, our approach is offered up with a grain of salt, knowing this isn't an ultimate how-to manual for success. Rather, it's a collection of thoughts designed to inspire anyone to think a little differently about how to prepare meals, adapt recipes to different environments, and strike a balance in the creative exploration of camp cooking.

This book is an evergreen helping hand for every camp cook's journey. Useful information and ideas are designed for beginners and seasoned cooks alike—from packing checklists to suggestions for making recipes your own, inspiration and opportunities are unwritten between the lines. Without concrete starting or end points, the satisfaction of self-sufficiency at your campsite is something to bask in, evolve, and master over a lifetime.

Preparing, cooking, and eating meals outdoors will be a new experience each and every time thanks to changing factors, such as the weather, your campsite, and who you're sharing it with. Look at these variables as opportunities to try new recipes, improvise on your favorites dishes, or add a surprise course. Many camp stews and grilled bratwurst plans have been delightfully derailed by luck in the form of a beautiful rainbow trout or two. Polenta or porridge dishes are easily modified with seasonal herbs and vegetables. Tuning in to what's bountiful in your region and season will yield special mealtime experiences made possible by a well-stocked pantry and basic camp cooking know-how.

In these pages, you'll find a breakdown of the camp cook's kitchen and pantry, some tried-and-true methods and suggestions, and a heaping handful of recipes inspired by our favorite camping memories with friends and family in beautiful landscapes. Many of these recipes are variations on familiar favorites created for their regions: the forest, the shore, and the desert.

Exploring old logging roads and discovering secret glacial lakes and winding mountain rivers conjure up a piney breeze and mossy, lush undergrowth. Berries and herbs are at home here. Finding snow-capped mountain views in the middle of August offers a good excuse to bridge the seasons with filling hot meals like Shishito Tomato Baked Eggs (page 70) or White Cheddar Beer Burgers (page 48).

At the shore, we fall in love time and time again with the mystery, simplicity, and abundance of our oceans, lakes, and rivers. Coal-Baked Oysters (page 74) pair beautifully with both misty fog and lazy afternoons, while Bonfire Mac and Cheese (page 77) warms your bones after a day spent in the cool, salty air. Here, there's a great expanse to discover, just like the sea itself.

In the desert, the steady incense of sunbaked sage riding a gentle wind is a perfect accent to reimagined cowboy classics. Meals like Chilaquiles with Crumbly Cheese (page 102) and White Bean Chili (page 113) arguably taste best under the shade of a wide-brimmed hat. Hot days and cold nights find their balance through the meals you pair them with.

At the end of the day, our philosophies can be summed up with these simple mantras:

▶ Do a lot with a little.
▶ Nourish yourself and your campmates.
▶ Any camp cook can create the best meal for the moment.
▶ Each meal is an opportunity to connect.

We hope this book empowers you to get out there and savor the great outdoors. Remember, every landscape and every season offers endless opportunities to connect, to explore, and to feed your body, mind, and soul.

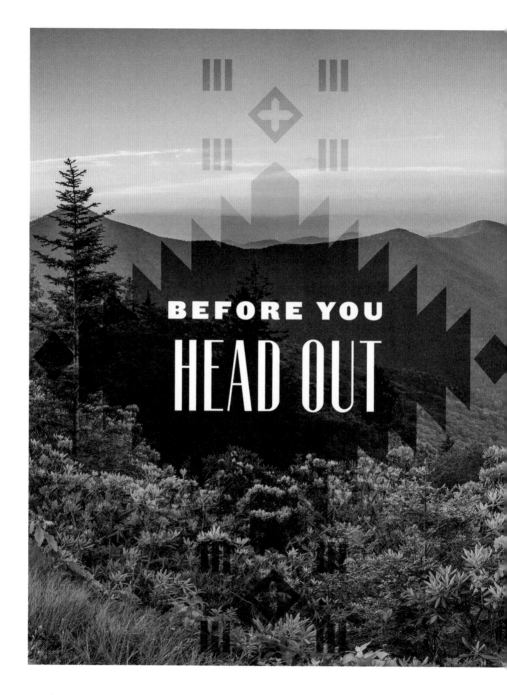

BEFORE YOU
HEAD OUT

THE CAMP KITCHEN

When packing your camp kitchen, keep in mind the balance of simplicity and preparedness. Camping can be a practice in minimalism, but that doesn't mean you should feel ill-equipped. Assuming you aren't backpacking, you can easily bring everything you need to set up a highly functional camp kitchen without feeling bogged down by all the *stuff*. Striking this balance will allow for simpler camping trips, more confident cooking, and an appreciation of utility that yields delicious, nourishing meals. The recipes in this book are designed to be made using a few essential tools and an efficient use of space.

When stocking up, first consider your heat source. Cooking over a campfire is our preferred method, but before embarking on any trip, check the local fire danger warnings and campfire regulations (they change with every season and, in some places, daily) and be confident in your safety precautions—we always have a bucket and shovel at the campsite. As far as firewood goes, the rule of thumb is to "buy it where

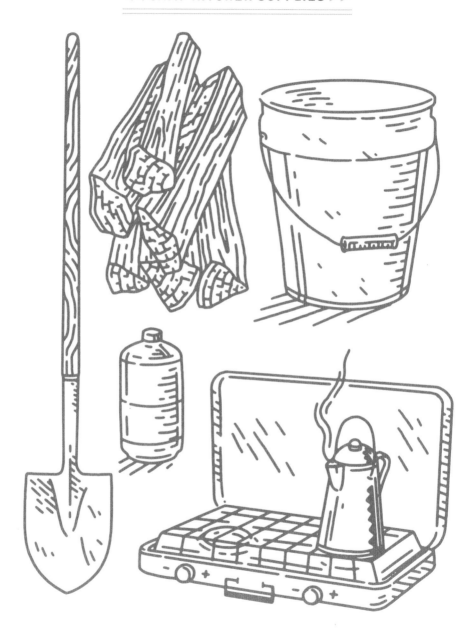

you burn it," as invasive species can often hitch a ride on out-of-town logs.

A good, double-burner propane camp stove is worth the investment and will last a lifetime. Anything in this book can be prepared with a camp stove and without a campfire. There are also many types of backpacking stoves on the market—compact, single-burner stoves that we often use on the side when a bonus heat source is needed. Test your camp stove before you head out and become confident with changing fuel canisters. Even if you plan to cook over the fire, it's wise to bring a camp stove in case of an unforeseen storm, high winds, or damp wood. Always pack an extra canister of fuel. Remember, just because you have a campfire doesn't mean you should feel pressured to cook everything on it—it's easier to set up a stove to boil water for pasta or heat the kettle for coffee.

THE ESSENTIALS

1. ROLL-UP OR FOLDABLE CAMP TABLE

2. CAMP COOKWARE

Pots and Pans

- ▶ Cast-iron skillets (one small or medium and one large)
- ▶ Dutch oven or a heavy-bottomed medium pot with lid
- ▶ Kettle

Cooking Utensils

- ▶ All-purpose chef's knife
- ▶ Paring knife
- ▶ Spatula
- ▶ Nesting bowls for mixing
- ▶ Tongs
- ▶ Wooden spoon
- ▶ Two cutting boards

Campfire and Stove Tools

- ▶ Camp stove and fuel
- ▶ Grill grate
- ▶ Waterproof matches
- ▶ Hot mitt or pot holder

3. SERVING AND CLEANUP

▶ Mugs, plates, and bowls

▶ Cutlery

▶ Scrubbing brush or sponge

▶ Dish towels

▶ Biodegradable dish soap

4. SUGGESTED

▶ Corkscrew

▶ Bottle opener

▶ Can opener

▶ Aluminum foil

▶ Measuring cups and spoons

▶ Grater or rasp-style grater

▶ Small strainer

▶ Meat thermometer

▶ Potato masher

▶ French press or teapot

▶ Oyster knife

▶ Collapsible tub for dishwashing

THE CAMP PANTRY

No matter what's on the menu, having a well-stocked pantry of staples is both necessary and empowering. Knowing you have everything you need at your campsite gives you freedom to go off script, modify any of our recipes, or create something spontaneous with that wild-caught fish. Of course, don't try to bring your entire home kitchen pantry. Instead, pick a handful of essential spices and condiments, and opt for small, refillable containers that seal tightly. Be sure to label each item, then organize your supplies into larger carryall containers with your kitchen tools, cookware, and serveware. We recommend using large storage bins with locking lids.

Oils and Fats

Pack ample olive oil, ghee, and another high-heat oil like safflower, grapeseed, canola, lard, or avocado. To elevate your dishes, bring a small container of aromatic, flavorful extra-virgin olive oil to drizzle on a sandwich or improvise in a dressing with wild herbs.

Salt

Opt for flaky sea salt as your all-purpose camp salt. We like Maldon from England, or Jacobsen from our neighbors in coastal Oregon. Keep a small container of kosher salt for pasta water and cast-iron cleaning.

Peppercorns

Pepper should always be freshly ground when needed so the flavors shine. Invest in a small refillable peppermill and keep your camp pantry stocked with whole black or a medley of peppercorns.

Dried Herbs and Spices

Bring what you like to use at home. We fill small containers with staples like paprika, red pepper flakes, cumin, and coriander. Small quantities of dried herbs, such as sage, oregano, dill, thyme, and tarragon, are nice to have at the ready.

Canned Tomatoes

Canned tomatoes are a go-to pinch-hitter when you need to throw something together quickly, like when you add an extra day to your camping trip and are running a little low on food. They easily marry odds and ends in a way that doesn't feel tossed together. We like peeled or crushed San Marzano tomatoes best.

Canned or Dried, Presoaked Beans

Beans are versatile and filling, making them a staple of camp cooking! We always have extra in our pantry, usually heirloom varietals like cassoulet and Christmas lima, but tried-and-true garbanzo, cannellini, pinto, and butter beans are great.

Grains, Flours, and Baking Ingredients

Even though there's very little baking going on at any given campsite, a few baking-aisle essentials will come in handy. Pack a small jar of granulated or raw sugar for desserts, dressings, and marinades. Flours make occasional appearances in our recipes, but you can often measure out what's needed before you leave. Our Blackberry and Herb Pancake batter (page 36) can be premeasured and mixed at home, removing the need to haul two types of flour or baking powder around. Invest in a small bottle of vanilla extract as a permanent fixture in your camp pantry—it's not essential, but having some on hand will enable you to take any impromptu sweet treat to the next level. Cornmeal and quinoa are great camping grains because of their quick cook times and unfussy preparation methods. Rolled oats are a reliable camping breakfast staple, and we recommend keeping a few servings in your pantry bin.

Pantry Produce

Garlic, onion, and shallot are essentials in our recipes. Bring more than you think you'll need and keep them dry and cool. Have lemons and limes for zesting, juicing, and finishing. Fresh ginger is always nice, even if just for tea. It's our habit to grab a big handful of mixed fresh herbs, such as dill, thyme, mint, chives, sage, tarragon, basil, and rosemary, for every camping trip.

Dairy

Always pack plenty of salted butter. A tub of good, plain Greek yogurt is a flexible, efficient camp companion that can be served with granola and fruit for breakfast, mixed into flatbread dough, or dolloped on a chili or stew. We always have cheese in our coolers even if just for an afternoon snack with salami, olives, or fruit spread. A small block of Cheddar, a good chunk of Parmesan, and some melting cheese, such as mozzarella, will go a long way. Take care when packing your eggs!

SKILLS AND CARE

Building skills is integral to camping. After plenty of practice, things like setting up camp, building the perfect fire, timing meal prep, and quickly packing out will come naturally.

Use this section as a starting point, and take what we provide as helpful guidelines rather than mandates—except, of course, cast-iron care. That's nonnegotiable! Here are a few guidelines, tips, and tricks that we've found success with over the years.

Types of Fire and Heat

One of the greatest camping skills you can learn is how to use the tools you have to create the heat you need. Campfire cooking is flexible and adaptable: For high heat, put your skillets and pots on a grill grate or place directly on top of hot coals. For medium heat or grilling, a grill grate placed toward one side of a hot fire will do. For low heat, place your skillet off to the far side of the fire. The hot rocks surrounding your fire can even double as a warming plate. Whatever you're cooking, know the type of heat you need before you build your fire.

SNACK FIRE: A small, efficient fire that lights quickly and burns with full flames and fleeting high heat, perfect for toasting or charring. Around kindling, build a teepee structure with logs or branches and burn until the structure falls. Place your kettle, pot, or skillet in the center and keep adding twigs to increase or prolong the heat.

COOKING FIRE: Larger than a snack fire and used when you plan to cook more or stay awhile. This is a strong fire that has a good, continuous burn. Depending on what method you like, you can build a larger teepee fire or use the log cabin method. To use it for cooking, place two green logs on either side of the fire or in the shape of a *V* (4 inches [10 cm] apart at one end and about 7 inches [17 cm] at the other).

COALS: Use a log cabin method to create a deep bed of coals, great for Dutch ovens and grilling or roasting meat. To create a log cabin fire, place two of your largest pieces of wood at the bottom, horizontally. Next, layer two pieces of wood on top of them vertically. Looking from above, you'll have created a #. Continue to build your log cabin, placing kindling and tinder at the base to light. Remember to get your fire going about an hour before you want to cook so the coals have plenty of time to burn down and get hot. A snack fire (see facing page) can even yield hot coals if fed well and maintained long enough!

FIELD MEASURING

It's not always realistic to carefully measure exact amounts of ingredients while you're in the backcountry, and in most cases, a good estimate will do just fine. Before you head out, practice measuring a teaspoon and then a tablespoon in your hand, making note of how it looks and feels. If you get the hang of this, you'll never need to pack measuring spoons!

QUICK CAMPSITE MEASUREMENTS

- ▶ "A big pinch" = ¼ teaspoon
- ▶ 4 "big pinches" = 1 teaspoon
- ▶ Fills the center of your palm = 1 tablespoon
- ▶ Coffee spoon = 1 teaspoon
- ▶ Dinner spoon = 1 tablespoon
- ▶ Standard coffee mug = 1 cup [240 ml]

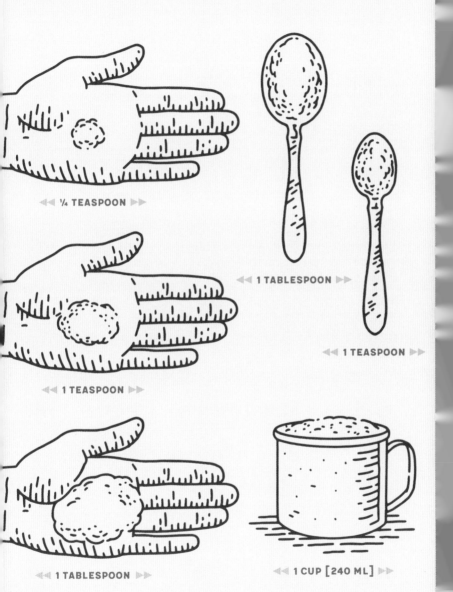

¼ TEASPOON

1 TABLESPOON

1 TEASPOON

1 TEASPOON

1 TABLESPOON

1 CUP [240 ML]

"Camp Clean"

Part of the beauty of camp cooking is accepting a little dirt, grit, and grease. Become comfortable with the concept of things being "camp clean," which to us generally means "clean enough." Do what you can to minimize the use of water for cleanup, and employ a scrub brush and dish towel rather than paper towels. Dispose of food scraps and dishwater responsibly to avoid any unwanted campsite visitors, and always use sparing amounts of biodegradable soap.

Cast-Iron Care

Cooking with cast iron provides better distribution of heat and regulation of temperature than other metals, and we find that the flavors of campfire cooking are enhanced when using this type of skillet. Cast iron can withstand white-hot coals, licking flames, and nearly unending use. With proper care, these skillets will last well beyond a lifetime and become cherished family heirlooms.

The term *seasoning* refers to a layer of carbonized oil that protects the cast iron and provides an ideal, naturally nonstick cooking surface. Brand-new cast irons require some time to develop this, but regular use and the right cleaning methods will ensure that you'll develop a good seasoning on your skillets. Most importantly, never use soap on any cast iron. Soap will break down the seasoning and expose the metal to oxidation and rust, which could ruin a perfectly good skillet. If soap is accidentally used, don't panic—just give the cast iron a good seasoning with a high-heat oil, like grapeseed oil, lard, or avocado oil.

Some cooks swear by never washing cast iron at all, but there are methods to safely remove messes without damaging the seasoning or the pan. After cooking, pour off extra grease for disposal and wipe or scrape out any food bits that easily come off. Heat a small amount of water in the skillet, scraping caked-on food loose with a wooden spoon. For particularly stubborn messes, gentle abrasion with kosher salt and a soft sponge should do the trick. Always thoroughly dry your "clean" cast iron with heat and coat with a thin layer of oil before putting them away. If your well-seasoned cast iron looks clean enough after cooking something that's not too messy, take pleasure in cutting out a cleanup step.

THE
FOREST

BLACKBERRY AND HERB PANCAKES

SERVES 2 TO 4
Medium-high heat; flame or hot coals

Skillet pancakes are forgiving and flexible: It's easy to prepare all the elements ahead of time, and you can swap the flours for any desired alternative so long as the ratios are right. If you'd prefer buttermilk pancakes, you can easily add a dash of lemon juice or apple cider vinegar to regular milk and let it sit for about 3 minutes before incorporating into the batter. As always, for the perfect pancake, make sure your skillet is sizzling hot.

This quick compote takes advantage of fresh fruits, which are a real treat when cooked in their own juices, creating an intense, thick, delicious syrup. Depending on the time of year, you may want to swap blackberries for peaches, figs, raspberries, or some other seasonal fruit (or use frozen fruit if your favorites are out of season). Of course, there's almost nothing as good as late summer blackberries, especially when paired with fresh herbs, such as tarragon or thyme. We like to keep it chunkier rather than smooth, but feel free to play depending on the fruit. Enjoy as is for a tangier, herbaceous compote or sweeten with sugar or maple syrup.

GATHER

FOR THE BERRY COMPOTE

1 to 3 cups [120 to 360 g] fresh blackberries, depending on how much compote you want to make

Handful of chopped fresh tarragon or thyme

1 to 2 Tbsp honey or maple syrup (optional)

Lemon zest (optional)

FOR THE PANCAKE BATTER

1 cup [140 g] all-purpose flour

½ cup [55 g] rye flour or ½ cup [70 g] buckwheat flour

3½ tsp baking powder

1 tsp flaky sea salt

1¼ cups [300 ml] milk or buttermilk

3 Tbsp butter or coconut oil, melted

Dash of vanilla (optional)

1 egg

BEFORE YOU HEAD OUT

To make the berry compote ahead of time:
In a sauté pan or skillet over medium-low heat, begin to cook down the berries, stirring occasionally and breaking down with a fork, about 3 to 5 minutes. Next, add the fresh herbs. Continue cooking for 5 to 10 minutes, until a spoon scraped through your berry mix leaves a trail in the liquid that doesn't come back together straight away. Stir in the honey and lemon zest, if using. Store in an airtight container or jar and pack in your cooler.

To make the pancake batter ahead of time:
In a bowl, combine the flours, baking powder, and salt. Pack the dry ingredients in a resealable plastic container to mix with the rest of the ingredients at the campsite.

To prepare the full batter at home, continue by making a well in the flour mixture, and then add the milk, melted butter, vanilla (if using), and egg. Whisk until smooth. Store in an airtight container or jar and pack in your cooler.

◀◀ CONTINUED ▶▶

AT THE CAMPSITE

In a sauté pan or skillet on the cooler side of your fire, reheat the premade berry compote. Set aside and keep warm under a lid or aluminum foil, giving it a fresh stir before you pile it on your pancakes.

If you've prepared only the dry batter ingredients ahead of time, finish preparing the pancake batter by adding the dry ingredients to a mixing bowl, creating a well in the mixture, and adding the milk, melted butter, vanilla (if using), and egg. Whisk until smooth.

Heat your skillet or sauté pan to medium-high or high heat, adding a generous amount of butter or oil. Using a big spoon or mug as a scoop, pour about ¼ cup [60 ml] of the batter directly onto the skillet. Let cook undisturbed until bubbles start to form and pop after 1 or 2 minutes. Flip once to cook the other side.

Remove from the heat and either serve right away with a big scoop of berry compote, or reserve in another pan, covered, until the rest have been cooked. Be sure to add more oil or butter to the pan so your pancakes don't stick.

Serve with your choice of toppings, such as butter, lemon zest, honey, fresh fruit, or maple syrup.

TAKE IT FURTHER

If you're feeling fancy (or just have extra ricotta to use), try mixing a few spoonfuls of the compote in with a dollop of ricotta, or if you have extra honey whipped ricotta (page 100), use that, topped with berries.

SKILLET HASH WITH SAUSAGE AND EGGS

SERVES 4
Medium heat; flame or hot coals

Sometimes, a cool morning in the forest calls for a big heaping plate of potatoes, eggs, sausage, cheese, and veggies. Potatoes help stretch servings out if you have a lot of hungry campers, and everyone can make their plate their own with add-ons like sour cream, buttered toast, or even homemade ranch dressing. Cut your potatoes into small pieces to reduce the time they need to cook. With all the parts and pieces of this recipe, everyone can pitch in to help prepare. We like to do it all in one skillet and serve family-style with add-ons ready at the table.

◀◀ CONTINUED ▶▶

GATHER

High-heat oil, such as safflower or grapeseed

2 lb [910 g] small potatoes, such as fingerling or yellow potatoes, cut into ½ in [12 mm] dice

Dash of chili powder

Flaky sea salt and freshly ground pepper

1 Tbsp butter

4 to 6 links breakfast sausage, casings removed

2 bell peppers, chopped

1 small or medium onion, chopped

Large handful of leafy greens, such as chard or lacinato kale, chopped

1 large or 2 small tomatoes or tomatillos, roughly chopped

3 garlic cloves, minced

6 oz [170 g] melting cheese, such as Monterey Jack, Cheddar, mozzarella, or Oaxacan, grated

4 eggs

Hot sauce, cilantro, and sour cream, for topping (optional)

AT THE CAMPSITE

Heat oil in a large sauté pan or skillet and add the potatoes, tossing to coat with oil while seasoning with chili powder, salt, and pepper. Stir occasionally, allowing the potatoes to begin to crisp and brown on all sides, about 8 to 10 minutes. Next, push the potatoes to the cooler side of the pan. (It might take some skill to keep one side hotter and the other side just warm; if you're worried about the potatoes burning while you cook the rest, remove them from the skillet and set aside for later.)

Melt the butter and add the breakfast sausage, breaking it up into pieces. Cook for 2 to 3 minutes while stirring until it begins to brown.

Next, add in the bell peppers and onions, stirring occasionally for about 5 minutes or until soft. Next, add the greens, tomatoes, and garlic. Season with salt and pepper and continue to cook for another 5 minutes or so, stirring occasionally.

Once everything is cooked, stir the potatoes back in to let the flavors marry, sprinkling in half of the cheese to melt.

Decide how you want your eggs, and either crack them right into the pan with everything and the remaining cheese to create a scramble, or plate the vegetable-sausage mixture, add the remaining cheese, and then top with sunny-side-up eggs. Finish with hot sauce, cilantro, and sour cream, if desired.

TAKE IT FURTHER

For a simple variation on homemade ranch dressing, stir 1 Tbsp of our ranch seasoning (page 124) into ½ cup [120 g] of sour cream or Greek yogurt and dollop on top of everything.

FRIED GREENS
WITH BACON

SERVES 2
Medium-low heat; stove or coals

Sometimes you just want a little snack—maybe it's a few hours until dinner or you burned through lunch on that hike faster than you thought. Whatever the reason, we can all do with a few more greens in our lives. Whether on their own or as a side to your main, this simple cook-up works morning, noon, and night.

GATHER

2 to 4 slices of bacon, cooked or raw (see Note)

1 Tbsp ghee (see Note)

1 shallot, ½ leek, or ¼ onion, thinly sliced

2 garlic cloves, minced

½ summer squash or zucchini, sliced into thin half-moons

Flaky sea salt and freshly ground pepper

1 bunch baby broccoli

Hearty greens of choice, such as kale, collards, or chard, chopped

Manchego cheese, grated (optional)

AT THE CAMPSITE

Get your pan going over medium heat, whether you're using coals or a stove. If you're cooking the bacon, fry it on one side for 3 to 5 minutes, flip, and cook on the other side until crisped to your liking, about 3 to 5 minutes. Remove the bacon and set aside, chopping or tearing it into pieces once it cools.

In the bacon fat or ghee, add the shallot and garlic. Cook, stirring often, until they start to become translucent. Add the squash, season with salt and pepper, and cook down for about 5 minutes. Stir and, just when everything is soft, add the baby broccoli and chopped greens. Toss a lid on for a few seconds to help it steam. Remove the lid, stir, add the bacon, and plate it up. Sprinkle with cheese, if desired.

NOTE: If you don't want to use bacon, try adding some good salty cheese, like Halloumi or aged Cheddar. If you cook the bacon in your pan first, use the remaining bacon fat instead of ghee.

TAKE IT FURTHER

Put an egg on it! Cook everything up just the same and a few minutes before things are done, crack an egg in the middle and cook, covered, for a few minutes until set. Season with salt and pepper, and you're ready to eat.

ALPINE GRILLED CHEESE

SERVES 4
Medium heat; low flame or hot coals

The lunch boxes of Alpine mountaineers inspired this grilled cheese sandwich. Grainy mustard fills the nooks and crannies of thick sourdough bread, sizzled in mayonnaise on all sides. Sweet and tart apple slices balance out the fatty, robust cheeses. A blend of Cheddar and Gruyère melts beautifully—don't be afraid to let it ooze out the sides!

GATHER

2 to 4 Tbsp butter

3 Tbsp mayonnaise

8 thick slices of sourdough bread

About 3 Tbsp grainy mustard

4 oz [115 g] sharp white Cheddar cheese, grated or sliced

4 oz [115 g] Gruyère or Swiss cheese, grated or sliced

1 green apple, thinly sliced

TAKE IT FURTHER

Serve with a side of corni-chons, olives, thin slices of summer sausage, or your favorite cured meats. Make it your own with add-ons like smoked turkey, bacon, fig spread, or other cheeses.

AT THE CAMPSITE

Heat your sauté pan or skillet over medium heat on hot coals or a small fire and melt a dab of butter.

For each sandwich, spread about ½ tsp of mayonnaise on one side of two slices of bread and sizzle mayonnaise-side down to create the interior texture for your sandwich. Once golden brown, transfer the bread mayonnaise-side up to a work surface for assembly. Slather each slice with about ½ tsp of grainy mustard. Add a quarter of the Cheddar and Gruyère and a few apple slices to one of the bread slices and top with the other toasted sourdough slice, mustard-side down.

Slather about ½ tsp of mayonnaise on the top of the sandwich. Add another dab of butter to the hot pan. Gently place your sandwich in the pan, mayonnaise-side down. Cover with a lid or another pan to help the cheese melt, if you like; otherwise, press down evenly with your spatula to help everything adhere. Sizzle for 3 to 5 minutes or until browned to perfection. Spread another ½ tsp of mayonnaise on top of the sandwich and flip, cooking for another 3 to 5 minutes, until the bread is golden brown and the cheese is visibly melty. Remove from the heat, cut into oozy triangles, and enjoy hot. Repeat with the remaining bread and toppings to make 3 more sandwiches.

SIMPLE MUSHROOM SHAKSHUKA

SERVES 4
Medium heat; low flame or coals

An easy one-pan dish that's filling, savory, and satisfying, shakshuka is great for breakfast, brunch, or dinner and can easily feed a crowd. Adapt for additional servings with an egg per person. Traditionally, shakshuka is a dish where eggs are poached in a spicy tomato sauce and served with bread for dipping. We love adding greens, cheese, green onions, or any extra veggies we need to use up (especially on the last day). Scoop it up with bread, eat it straight from the pan, or serve it in bowls with a dollop of Greek yogurt.

GATHER

3 Tbsp olive oil

1 onion, finely diced

1 tsp cumin

½ tsp cinnamon

Pinch of red pepper flakes

1 to 2 cups [60 to 120 g] diced mushrooms

Flaky sea salt and freshly ground pepper

One 14 oz [400 g] can diced tomatoes

4 eggs

Chopped fresh parsley

Crusty bread, for serving

TAKE IT FURTHER

A dollop of Greek yogurt on top can help balance the spice and acidity, or a can of garbanzo beans can make the meal even more substantial. Try serving with our Skillet Flatbreads (page 105) to sop up every last drop and morsel.

AT THE CAMPSITE

Light your fire and let it burn down to medium heat, setting up a grill grate, or set up a gas stove and turn the flame to medium heat.

In your sauté pan or skillet, add the oil and onion, sautéing for about 5 minutes until it starts to soften. Next, stir in your spices, let them cook until fragrant, and then add the mushrooms. Add salt and pepper and sauté, stirring occasionally, until the mushrooms are soft, about 6 minutes. Add the tomatoes and mix everything together. Immediately cover and shift your skillet to a cooler part of the fire so it can simmer for about 20 minutes, stirring occasionally as the sauce thickens. Taste and adjust the seasoning as needed.

Once you feel good about the sauce, it's time for the eggs. Use your spoon to make four evenly spaced indentations in the sauce. In each, crack an egg, and put the lid back on to cook for another 5 to 6 minutes, or until the eggs are done to your liking—we like the whites set and the yolk still runny. Remove from the heat, sprinkle with fresh parsley, and serve with crusty bread.

WHITE CHEDDAR BEER BURGERS

SERVES 4
Medium to medium-high heat;
stove, flame, or hot coals

These hearty burgers are an indulgent twist on a classic. Good brioche, a sharp, earthy Cheddar, pan-sizzled mustard, and onions sautéed in beer create robust layers of flavor on top of smash-burger style beef patties. Our secret sauce is a variation on the classic fry sauce beloved by burger stands all over the country. We skip the pickles for the sake of cooler space, but feel free to add any burger fixings you prefer. Crack open a cold beverage and get ready for your campmates to ask for seconds. You might want to pack extra napkins for this!

GATHER

FOR THE SECRET SAUCE

¼ cup [60 g] mayonnaise

2 Tbsp ketchup

1 Tbsp apple cider vinegar

Flaky sea salt and freshly ground black pepper

FOR THE BURGERS

1¼ lb [570 g] 80% lean ground beef

2 Tbsp butter

1 large yellow onion, diced

Flaky sea salt and freshly ground pepper

One 12 oz [360 ml] can session beer, like a pilsner, Kölsch, lager, or light ale— we like Rainier

Yellow or Dijon mustard

6 to 8 oz [170 to 230 g] aged white Cheddar cheese, such as Tillamook or Kerrygold Dubliner Irish Cheddar, sliced

Mayonnaise

4 brioche hamburger buns

1 large ripe heirloom tomato, sliced

Butterhead, romaine, or iceberg lettuce leaves

Ketchup

BEFORE YOU HEAD OUT

To make the secret sauce ahead of time: Combine the mayonnaise, ketchup, and apple cider vinegar in a small bowl until evenly incorporated. Grind in a liberal amount of black pepper, stirring until thoroughly speckled, and add a pinch of sea salt. Store in an airtight jar or squeeze bottle in your cooler until it's burger time.

To further minimize campsite prep, divide the ground beef into four even portions, about 5 oz [140 g] each. Loosely form balls, without pressing too firmly. Wrap with plastic and store in your cooler.

◀◀ CONTINUED ▶▶

AT THE CAMPSITE

To make the burgers:

Remove your ground beef balls from the cooler a half hour ahead of cooking to reach ambient temperature.

Bring a large sauté pan or skillet to medium heat, either on your camp stove or over the edge of hot coals. Melt 1 Tbsp of the butter in the pan and add the onions, seasoning with salt and pepper. Stir occasionally as the onion begins to brown. Add a splash of beer directly to the pan, scraping up any browned bits as the onions soften. Let the onions cook for 10 to 15 minutes, adding splashes of beer here and there until the onions are uniformly soft and brown. Remove from the pan and set aside.

Add half of the reserved onions to the prepared secret sauce, stirring to incorporate. We often add a tiny splash of beer right into the sauce too. Adjust the seasoning with salt and pepper and set aside.

Season the ground beef balls with sea salt and freshly ground pepper. With your pan now reaching medium-high heat, add a dab of butter and place a beef ball squarely on top. With your spatula and without haste, press down with a smearing motion a few times, spreading the patty onto the hot surface in all directions. Cook for 1 or 2 minutes, depending on your heat, until the smeared edges become crispy and browned. Add a squirt of mustard to the patty, then flip it over mustard-side down. Immediately add a slice or two of cheese and cook for another 2 to 3 minutes. Add a splash of beer to the pan, if desired, and cover with a lid (or another skillet) to help the cheese melt fully.

Apply a smear of mayonnaise to both sides of the brioche buns and press onto the hot skillet to toast until the patty finishes cooking.

To assemble:
Top the bottom bun with the secret sauce, followed by the cheeseburger patty, some beer onions, a slice of tomato, a big leaf or two of lettuce, and the top half of the bun, slathered with secret sauce, ketchup, and any other condiments you'd like. Serve immediately to the hungriest camper and repeat with the remaining ingredients to keep the assembly line going.

PAN PORK CHOPS WITH GOAT CHEESE

SERVES 4
High heat; hot coals

For a chilly lakeside night spent in the mountains, this protein-rich and decadent dinner will guarantee a good night's sleep. Juicy panfried pork chops smothered with goat cheese might seem like a big undertaking for a camp meal, but it's simple as can be and comes together quickly.

GATHER

2 Tbsp butter

1 bunch fresh sage leaves

Four 6 oz [170 g] bone-in pork chops, at ambient temperature

6 oz [170 g] plain goat cheese

Flaky sea salt and freshly ground pepper

AT THE CAMPSITE

Heat a large cast-iron sauté pan or skillet over high heat, over or directly on hot coals. Melt the butter in the pan, sprinkle in a few sage leaves, and add your pork chops, sizzling in the butter for 3 to 5 minutes until you see the edges browning. Flip the pork chops and place a few leaves of sage on top while the other side cooks, an additional 3 to 5 minutes depending on thickness. (Check for doneness by giving the pork chops a poke—medium-cooked pork will feel like the fleshy part of your hand between your thumb and forefinger when you press your thumb and middle finger together. If you have a meat thermometer in your camp kitchen, check that the internal temperature reaches at least 145°F [63°C].) Remove the pork chops from the pan and set aside to rest.

Plate each pork chop with goat cheese and freshly chopped sage on top. Sprinkle with salt and pepper to finish.

SKILLET SMASHED POTATOES WITH SAGE BUTTER

SERVES 4
High heat; hot coals

An unfussy and filling dinner on its own, or an easy side to any other main dish, these potatoes are nearly impossible to mess up. They're boiled and then panfried to create a crispy texture encasing soft, fluffy interiors. Make them your own with your favorite herbs or spices—we like to treat them as a vehicle for sage butter, as described here.

GATHER

2 lb [910 g] small potatoes, such as fingerling or yellow

2 Tbsp butter

1 bunch fresh sage leaves

Flaky sea salt and freshly ground pepper

TAKE IT FURTHER

If mashed potatoes are more your style, and if you camp with a potato masher, add 3 Tbsp of butter to the hot pot of boiled potatoes and mash. Add about 3 oz [85 g] goat cheese and ½ cup [120 ml] milk or cream and continue to mash, seasoning with salt, pepper, and sage or other herbs.

Turn this dish into a meal with classic baked potato add-ons: sour cream, Cheddar cheese, green onions, bacon bits, or ranch seasoning (page 124).

AT THE CAMPSITE

Bring a pot of salted water to a boil and drop in your whole potatoes, skin on, boiling until you can easily stick a fork through. Drain and set aside.

Meanwhile, heat a large cast-iron pan over high heat, over or directly on hot coals.

Melt the butter in the pan with some of the sage leaves. Add the boiled potatoes to the skillet and stir to coat in butter. Next, hold the pan steady with a hot mitt and gently smash the potatoes with the back of a spatula, flattening them to brown and panfry in the butter. Season with salt and pepper. When the edges are crispy and browned, remove from the heat and serve right out of the skillet.

Heap onto your plate with freshly chopped sage and call it a day.

BAKED SWEET APPLES WITH HONEY

SERVES 4
Medium heat; coals

Naturally sweet, savory, and completely comforting, warm baked apples are always a treat. We love them in the fall when the new crop is in, but enjoy this recipe all year long. If you don't have apples, or prefer to save them for your hike, try peaches, pears, or any other seasonal fruit you might be used to seeing in a pie. Serve warm and don't be shy about leftovers in the morning with a strong cup of coffee.

GATHER

Dash of cinnamon

Dash of nutmeg

Dash of clove

Pinch of salt

½ cup [110 g] ghee or salted butter

3 to 4 Tbsp honey

3 baking apples, such as Granny Smith, seeded and sliced into rounds

Handful of other fruits such as berries or sliced pears (optional)

Juice of ½ orange

Handful of crushed walnuts

Mason Jar Whipped Cream (page 121)

BEFORE YOU HEAD OUT

To make it simple, you can premix your spices so you're bringing only one container instead of four. Combine the cinnamon, nutmeg, clove, and salt in an airtight container and label for later.

AT THE CAMPSITE

Start a fire and burn it down for about an hour so you've got a consistent medium heat. Put a grill grate over the top so you can cook a little more like a stovetop (alternatively, bring the fire down to a lower heat, spread the coals, and cook directly atop the coals).

Place your cast-iron skillet over the grill and melt your ghee and honey. Add the spices, cooking until they become fragrant, for about a minute, then add the apple slices and any other fruit you're using in a single layer, stirring to evenly coat in butter and honey. Add a generous squeeze of orange juice and a handful of walnuts, stir, and cover with a lid for a few minutes. Uncover, stir, and continue to cook until you can easily pierce them with a fork. Add the rest of the orange juice, stirring as it reduces. Remove from the heat and serve with fresh Mason Jar Whipped Cream.

◄◄ CONTINUED ►►

TAKE IT FURTHER

Toast your crushed walnuts in a skillet over the fire before sprinkling on your baked apples. There's nothing better than a freshly toasted walnut, still a little warm. Also, grate some fresh orange zest, or any citrus you have, straight into the pan to brighten things up. You can also have a lot of fun mixing up flavors and textures in this dish by swapping walnuts for whatever you have on hand, or switching up the spices for whatever feels most seasonally appropriate.

WILDERNESS TEA

Traditionally known as a tisane (pronounced *ti-zan*), this is one of our favorite ways to use up extra herbs from cooking, but the method works just the same for whatever you use. Generally speaking, tisanes are an infusion of herbs, fruit, bark, flowers, or spices steeped (or boiled) in hot water. Here are some possible components:

Leaf Tisanes
lemon verbena
peppermint
mint
juniper
rosemary

Flower Tisanes
rose hips
lavender
chamomile

Fruit Tisanes
hibiscus (technically a flower but with a tart, berrylike flavor)
raspberry
citrus

Spiced Tisanes
cardamom
fennel
caraway
star anise
cinnamon

Whatever flavor profile you create, it's guaranteed to warm your belly as you sip it fireside.

◄◄ CONTINUED ►►

◄◄ LEAF TISANES ►►

◄◄ FRUIT TISANES ►►

◄◄ FLOWER TISANES ►►

◄◄ SPICED TISANES ►►

GATHER

Handful of herbs, spices, fruit, bark, or flowers to steep

TAKE IT FURTHER

Try making more elaborate blends! Tisanes are full of essential oils and nutrients, so you can read up on the health benefits of different herbs, fruits, and barks to see what strikes your fancy.

BEFORE YOU HEAD OUT

If you already know your favorite blends, premix a few combinations so they're ready for the road. We like to store ours in mason jars, but since you're using fresh herbs, fruit, and other ingredients, it might be nice to play this one by ear—using either fresh or dried ingredients. As a reminder, forage for edibles only if you're experienced in plant identification and safe foraging. And remember: The fresher the ingredients, the better your tisane.

AT THE CAMPSITE

Over coals, fill your kettle or pot with enough water for however many mugfuls of tea you'd like (or enough to fill your French press).

Next, rinse the herbs, making sure they're extra clean and there isn't any dirt or muck stuck to them. Stalks are fine! Once the water has boiled, grab the other pot or French press, add your herbs, and pour boiling water over everything. Let steep for at least 5 minutes and serve warm.

If you're using a French press or teapot, you don't have to worry too much about straining. However, if you threw those herbs in a pot and waited (like we usually do), you'll either want to use the lid to strain or a small strainer when pouring to serve.

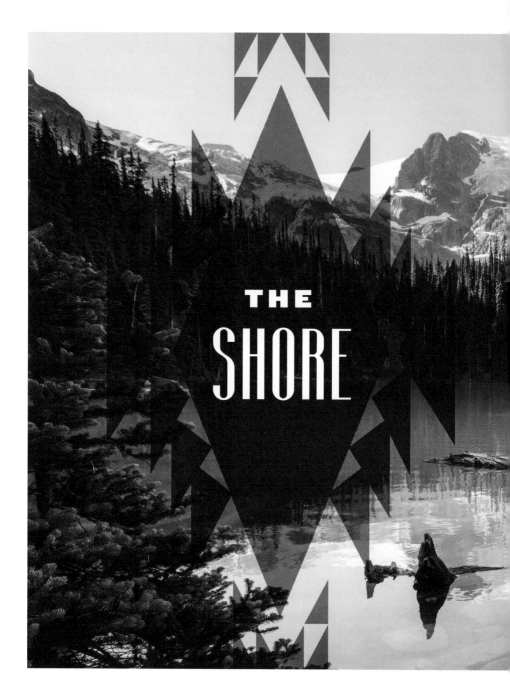

THE
SHORE

OVERNIGHT OATS WITH BERRIES

SERVES 2
No heat

This breakfast staple can be prepared completely at home or at camp. We like overnight oats because they're simple, they provide nutrients and energy for the day, and they're a great base for plenty of other flavors and textures—sweet, savory, spicy, creamy, chunky, crunchy. The general idea is to put some grains (we like oats) in a mason jar, add any other dry things you might like (coconut, carob, nuts), toss in spices and sweetener, fill to just covered with a liquid of choice (usually dairy or nondairy milk), seal, and let it wait until morning. Open, stir it up, add something fresh, and you're ready to go. Our recipe will walk you through the steps half at home, half at the campsite.

GATHER

½ cup [50 g] rolled oats or gluten-free grain of choice

¼ cup [13 g] shredded coconut

1 Tbsp chia seeds

Handful of mixed nuts and seeds, unsalted

Dash of cinnamon

Add-ins, such as a spoonful of nut butter, yogurt, fruit, cacao powder, honey, and goji berries (optional)

1 cup [240 ml] vanilla nondairy milk, or more as needed

Fresh berries or fruit

BEFORE YOU HEAD OUT

Premix as many servings of overnight oats as you'll want for your camping trip. We like to fill one mason jar per person.

Grab two 16 oz [480 ml] mason jars with lids. Since this recipe is *really* forgiving, you can eyeball your amounts, but if you want to measure it out: Add ¼ cup [25 g] of the rolled oats, 2 Tbsp of the shredded coconut, a heaping teaspoon of the chia seeds, nuts, cinnamon, and any other dry ingredients you want to each jar. Screw on the lids, give them a shake, and they're ready to go for the campsite.

AT THE CAMPSITE

The night before (or at least 2 hours before) mealtime, add about ½ cup [120 ml] of the nondairy milk to each mason jar, or enough to cover all the oats and other ingredients. Stir, seal, and keep them in your cooler overnight.

In the morning, stir the oats and add fresh fruit, yogurt, or whatever other toppings you want. Enjoy right out of the jar for easy cleanup.

◄◄ CONTINUED ►►

TAKE IT FURTHER

Go decadent and make "healthy" chocolate peanut butter oats by adding a handful of dark chocolate chips and a spoonful of peanut butter. We also love to add plenty of unexpected spices—such as nutmeg or cardamom—and lots of seasonal fruits.

If you aren't one for cold cereals, soak everything overnight and heat it up in the morning over low heat, adding your toppings at the end.

BLUE CORN AND SWEET POTATO BREAKFAST TACOS

SERVES 4
Medium heat; flame or coals

Everybody loves a breakfast taco. Appropriate and welcome no matter the region or season, they're wildly versatile and decidedly delicious. If you feel inspired to change it up, use this recipe as a guideline: Toast your corn or flour tortilla and then fill it with a mixture of eggs, meat, veggies, cheese, or leftovers. Serve with your favorite hot sauce or add-ons.

◄◄ CONTINUED ►►

GATHER

Olive oil or ghee

1 shallot or ¼ white onion, chopped

½ sweet potato, cut into ¼ in [6 mm] cubes

4 oz [115 g] goat cheese

4 eggs

1 tsp mustard

Flaky sea salt and freshly ground pepper

4 soft blue corn tortillas

Hot sauce

BEFORE YOU HEAD OUT

There's not much to do beforehand, but if you are making your own tortillas, you can prep those at home and store them in aluminum foil, warming them when you're ready to cook. If you want, you could also precook your sweet potatoes so you just have to warm them at camp. The advantage there is that you don't have to wait, but the trick is making sure they're warmed all the way through when your eggs are ready.

AT THE CAMPSITE

Light your fire and let it cook down for about an hour until you have a consistent medium heat.

In your cast iron over the grill, add the oil, shallot, and sweet potato. Stir often, cooking until they start to brown and soften, about 10 minutes (test the potatoes by poking them with the tip of your knife or fork).

Next, crumble in your goat cheese, crack in the eggs, and add a small scoop of good mustard. We like to lightly scramble everything up into a hash, but it's up to you how you like your eggs— fried, over-easy, or scrambled are probably best, though. Season with salt and pepper and set the pan aside.

Lay the tortillas out over the grill grate. Lightly toast on one side, flip, and warm the other side.

To assemble the tacos, either hold the tortilla in your hand, scooping the egg mixture in, or make up two at a time, open-face, with the egg mixture on top. Add some hot sauce and enjoy.

TAKE IT FURTHER

Get a little fancy and make it into a gordita: Place a corn tortilla in the pan, add some cheese, and as it starts to melt, top it with another tortilla. Flip once and fill just as you would a regular taco. If you go this route, you'll need 8 tortillas for 4 tacos.

SHISHITO TOMATO BAKED EGGS

SERVES 2
Medium heat; stove or flame

This dish of eggs poached in a sauce of tomatoes, peppers, and aromatics is heavily spiced, soul-wakening, and easy enough to make for two campers or double or triple for a crowd. Feel free to swap in whatever veggies and spices you have on hand—we often use a mild curry and smoky cumin, but other spices such as smoked paprika, garam masala, or coriander work well—and for extra protein, you can add sausage or beans. The most important thing is to make sure you let the tomato sauce thicken before adding your eggs. It can be tough to wait, but it makes all the difference. To take it to the next level, we highly recommend topping this dish with a briny cheese, such as barrel-aged feta.

GATHER

1 to 2 Tbsp olive oil

2 zucchinis, cubed or diced

Handful of shishito peppers, stemmed

1 garlic clove, minced

Flaky sea salt and freshly ground pepper

One 14 oz [400 g] can crushed tomatoes

2 tsp curry

1 tsp cumin

1 red onion, cut into thin half-moons

4 eggs

Handful of parsley, chopped

Feta crumbles, for topping (optional)

Crusty baguette or Skillet Flatbreads (page 105), for serving (optional)

BEFORE YOU HEAD OUT

If you want to save some time, chop your veggies at home and store them in a plastic bag or mason jar so they're ready to go.

AT THE CAMPSITE

Heat the olive oil in your skillet over a medium-heat fire. Add the zucchinis, shishito peppers, and garlic and season with salt and pepper. The idea is to slowly cook down your zucchini and peppers until tender and starting to brown, which should take about 5 minutes. If you're using vegetables that have different cooking times, cook them one by one, starting with those that take the longest, adding the others as you go, so that they all finish at about the same time.

Move to a lower heat portion of the fire and, in the same pan, add your tomatoes and spices. Stir to combine and allow to simmer for 1 minute. Scatter the red onion around the skillet and season with salt and pepper.

Now it's time for the eggs. With a wooden spoon, create four small, evenly spaced indentations in the veggies. Crack an egg into each. Return your pan to the fire and continue to cook, undisturbed, until the egg whites have set and the yolks remain runny. Garnish with freshly chopped parsley and feta (if using) and enjoy family-style right out of the skillet. For a more filling meal, serve with a crusty baguette.

CHARRED CORN SALAD WITH SPICES

SERVES 4
Medium heat; flame or hot coals

If you're already grilling, you might as well throw on a few ears of corn to create this delicious side salad. It pairs beautifully with tacos, Spicy Stuffed Whole Fish (page 85), Coal-Baked Oysters (page 74), or White Cheddar Beer Burgers (page 48). We love to give this salad a kick with cayenne and fresh lime juice, but we'll use a premixed elote seasoning just as often.

GATHER

3 ears summer corn, shucked

Salted butter or ghee, for rubbing corn

Cayenne or elote seasoning (optional)

¼ red onion, finely chopped

Fresh lime juice

1 tsp olive oil

Flaky sea salt and freshly ground pepper

½ cup [60 g] crumbled queso fresco

⅓ to ½ cup [15 to 20 g] chopped fresh cilantro

BEFORE YOU HEAD OUT

You can make an elote seasoning blend if you want—we swear by the stuff: sea salt, dried chile pepper, Parmesan cheese, dried chipotle powder, citric acid, dried cilantro, and cumin powder. The ratios are going to be up to you and what you like, but test it out and see! That's half the fun.

AT THE CAMPSITE

Light a fire and let it burn down for about an hour until you have a consistent medium heat, placing an oiled grill grate on top.

Rub your corn with butter and season with cayenne, if desired, or just put it straight on the grill. Turn occasionally, letting the ears get some color, until slightly charred. It should be about 10 minutes, depending on your fire.

Let cool and then cut the kernels from the cob, transferring them to a large bowl. Add the red onion, lime juice, and oil and season with salt and pepper. Stir to combine and then gently mix in the queso and cilantro. Serve as a side salad, topper for tacos, or dip with some chips.

COAL-BAKED OYSTERS

SERVES 2
High heat; white-hot coals

There's nothing that conjures up a waterside campsite scene more than a beautiful bounty of oysters. Raw oysters are perfect for a hot day, but our smoky baked rendition warms bellies on a cold night. Savory, salty, and simple enough to cook up on a whim, oysters can be seasoned however you'd like—we favor Parmesan, garlic, and parsley—but all you really need is a good squeeze of lemon juice.

GATHER

1 dozen raw oysters, shucked (or as many as you'd like)

3 Tbsp butter

¼ cup [10 g] chopped fresh parsley, plus more for topping

1 garlic clove, minced

1 to 2 handfuls of grated Parmesan cheese, plus more for topping

Flaky sea salt and freshly ground black pepper

Hot sauce

Lemon slices

BEFORE YOU HEAD OUT

Grate the Parmesan before you go, storing as much as you think you may want for the trip in a mason jar. Don't forget an oyster knife! If you don't have one, a flat-head screwdriver works well too.

AT THE CAMPSITE

You have two choices here: Either set up a fire and let it burn down to coals, or light some charcoal and let the coals burn down until white hot, spreading them into an even layer.

Once you've shucked the oysters, keep them on ice until you're ready to cook.

In a pot, over low heat, add the butter, parsley, garlic, cheese, salt, pepper, and a dash of hot sauce. Stir a few times until fully melted and combined, then pull it off the heat.

Next, grab a cutting board and line up your shucked oysters. Spoon the butter mixture into each, filling to the top. Carefully place the filled oysters on the hot coals and let cook for 3 to 4 minutes; the edges will slightly frill when done. Pull them off, let cool for a minute, and top with a little more cheese, parsley, and a squeeze of lemon.

◄◄ CONTINUED ►►

TAKE IT FURTHER

Try different dressings, sauces, and toppings! This is where you can get wild and create magic with local ingredients, your imagination, and things you've tried at restaurants before. Champagne vinaigrette, white wine vinegar, shallots—as a rule of thumb, use an acid or vinegar for your base, pick an aromatic, and add something fresh to top it all off.

BONFIRE MAC AND CHEESE

SERVES 4
Medium-high heat; open flame, then coals

For a chilly shoreline evening, piping hot bowls of comforting mac and cheese is a guaranteed crowd-pleaser. Our version is easy to make in one pot with minimal steps. Mixing hard and soft cheeses yields an oozy consistency that works with forks or spoons. Smoked Gouda, cayenne, and lots of fresh ground black pepper give this dish a smoky kick, making each bite more warming than the last. Whip this one up quickly and enjoy fireside at dusk.

◄◄ CONTINUED ►►

GATHER

One 16 oz [455 g] package of your favorite dried pasta, such as bow tie, cavatappi, or classic macaroni

½ cup [110 g] salted butter

1 cup [240 ml] milk, or half-and-half for a richer sauce

2 cups [160 g] grated white Cheddar cheese

1 cup [80 g] grated smoked Gouda

1 cup [30 g] grated Parmesan cheese, plus more for serving

1 tsp salt

1 tsp freshly ground black pepper, plus more for serving

½ to 1 tsp cayenne pepper, depending on desired heat

BEFORE YOU HEAD OUT

Feel free to grate your cheeses ahead of time, measuring out the needed quantities and storing in an airtight container. Freshly grated cheese is best, but prepping a day ahead will save time fireside and won't compromise flavor.

AT THE CAMPSITE

Bring a large pot of salted water to a boil over high heat, keeping in mind you'll need to create a bed of medium-hot coals later. To achieve this, keep your fire burning hot and compact by adding logs or branches as you go, allowing coals to develop at the center.

Add the pasta and cook just shy of al dente— the pasta will continue to cook with the cheese sauce. Drain, reserving 1 cup [240 ml] of pasta water, and quickly add the butter to the pasta, tossing to prevent the pasta from sticking. In the same pot, add the milk, cheeses, salt, black pepper, and cayenne and stir vigorously to combine.

Cover with a lid, a skillet, or aluminum foil, moving the pot onto low heat to keep warm. Allow the cheeses to completely melt and the flavors to marry, 10 to 15 minutes, stirring occasionally and seasoning with salt and pepper. If the sauce seems too thick, add a splash of pasta water and stir to incorporate.

Scoop heaping spoonfuls into deep bowls and top with plenty of fresh ground black pepper and extra Parmesan.

TAKE IT FURTHER

If you have a few strips of bacon to spare, dice and sauté them in a hot skillet and add the bacon bits right before serving. We're also big fans of adding cauliflower to mac and cheese—it adds nutrients without compromising flavor, and is a good way to create more servings if you're low on pasta. Steam florets of cauliflower in a skillet with butter to soften and brown, about 15 minutes, then combine with the pasta and cheese sauce.

SWEET AND SOUR STICKY WINGS

SERVES 4
High heat; hot coals

We believe that you can cook almost anything in your camp kitchen, and finger-licking bar fare is a fun and rewarding undertaking. We like to borrow ideas from our favorite restaurants and pubs and translate them to the camping environment. This recipe for chicken wings uses Thai ingredients to achieve deep, multifaceted flavors. We like to balance the heat, sweetness, and saltiness of these wings with our Crisp Cabbage Salad with Toasted Almonds (page 83). With much of the prep done ahead of time, this one can come together in a snap, whether on a warm afternoon in the shade or fireside on a chilly night.

GATHER

FOR THE SAUCE

¼ cup [60 ml] maple syrup

¼ cup [60 ml] soy sauce

2 Tbsp fish sauce

4 garlic cloves, minced

1 in [2.5 cm] piece fresh
ginger, minced

FOR THE WINGS

About 3 lb [1.4 kg] chicken
wings, flats, and drumettes

Kosher salt

1 Tbsp butter

Handful of roasted
peanuts, chopped

Handful of fresh cilantro,
chopped

1 lime, cut into wedges

BEFORE YOU HEAD OUT

To make the sauce ahead of time:
Combine the maple syrup, soy sauce, fish sauce, garlic, and ginger in a leak-proof jar. Whisk or seal tightly and shake until everything is incorporated, label the sauce, and pack in your cooler.

Cut out another step by preparing the chicken wings ahead of time. Pat dry with a paper towel, lightly salt on all sides, and seal in an airtight container or plastic bag. Keep cold and dry until it's time to cook.

AT THE CAMPSITE

To make the wings:
You'll want a well-established bed of hot coals with some flames for this one. Arrange a grill grate over hot coals and within reach of licking flames. Place your salted wings on the grill grate and cook, turning frequently, until the meat is firm to the touch and uniformly golden brown, 8 to 10 minutes.

Meanwhile, heat your cast-iron sauté pan or skillet over medium-high heat and melt the butter. Transfer the cooked wings to the pan, tossing them in the butter, and then add the sauce, constantly stirring to coat evenly. Remove from the heat once the sauce feels stickier. Toss with the peanuts right before plating, and top with cilantro and a lime wedge.

◀◀ CONTINUED ▶▶

TAKE IT FURTHER

Deglazing the cast-iron sauté pan with about half a beer will do two things: Help clean the pan and transform extra sauce into a glaze to pour over the wings when plating. Right after removing the wings from the pan, pour in 6 oz [180 ml] of pilsner, lager, or pale ale and scrape up the sauce and bits. Simmer for a few minutes to reduce.

To make this bar snack into a whole meal, serve the wings with a side of sticky rice, over a bed of our Crisp Cabbage Salad with Toasted Almonds (page 83), or alongside Campfire Grilled Pizza (page 110).

CRISP CABBAGE SALAD WITH TOASTED ALMONDS

SERVES 4
Medium heat; coals

This fresh, light dish is full of bright flavors and crisp textures. Quick to bring together, our easy cabbage salad pairs nicely with many other dishes. The dressing strikes a balance between acid and umami, and it's easy to tailor to your taste. A go-to salad dressing should be a permanent fixture in your cooler, and this one will keep for weeks. Even a simple salad makes use of the campfire with the addition of toasted almonds and sesame seeds. If done on their own, the toasted nuts and seeds in this dish are a good excuse to practice building a small snack fire (see page 28).

◄◄ CONTINUED ►►

GATHER

FOR THE SALAD DRESSING

¼ cup [60 ml] canola, safflower, or sunflower oil

1 Tbsp toasted sesame oil

3 Tbsp soy sauce

3 Tbsp rice wine vinegar or apple cider vinegar

1 Tbsp maple syrup or brown sugar

1½ in [4 cm] piece fresh ginger, minced

Freshly ground black pepper

FOR THE SALAD

1 head green or red cabbage (or half of each), cut into long, thin strips

1 bunch green onions, chopped

¼ cup [30 g] slivered almonds

2 Tbsp sesame seeds

Handful of fresh cilantro, chopped

Add-ons such as lime wedges, fresh grated ginger, or fried shallots (optional)

BEFORE YOU HEAD OUT

To make the salad dressing ahead of time:
Whisk together the oils, soy sauce, vinegar, maple syrup, ginger, and pepper in a leak-proof jar. Label and store in your cooler. This dressing will naturally separate, so shake the jar vigorously before serving.

AT THE CAMPSITE

To make the salad:
In a bowl, toss together the cabbage and dressing. Add the green onions and toss to incorporate, then set aside for a few minutes to allow the flavors to marry. If you have the cooler space, set the salad in your cooler to chill.

In a small sauté pan or skillet, quickly toast the almonds and sesame seeds over the fire until fragrant and golden, being careful not to burn.

Plate servings of the cabbage salad and top with the cilantro, toasted almonds, and sesame seeds. Try add-ons like a squeeze of lime, fresh grated ginger, or fried shallots, if desired.

SPICY STUFFED WHOLE FISH

SERVES 4

Medium heat; low flame or hot coals

An impressive one-dish meal that can feed a crowd, this whole stuffed fish is easy to make, versatile, and full of flavor. We use hot peppers, onion, lemon, and lots of fresh herbs, but you can stuff your fish with whatever ingredients you have on hand, and it can easily adapt to cook perfectly over different types of heat. Serve with crusty bread, a side of rice or salad, or more grilled veggies. We opt for Skillet Flatbreads (page 105) to really fill up.

If you aren't sure what kind of fish to use, ask your local monger, letting them know what you've got in mind, and requesting they scale and gut it for you.

◄◄ CONTINUED ►►

GATHER

**FOR THE MARINADE
(OPTIONAL, SEE NOTE)**

3 to 6 hot peppers

3 shallots, chopped

6 to 8 garlic cloves,
crushed or finely chopped

1½ in [4 cm] piece fresh
ginger, grated or finely
chopped

⅓ cup [80 ml] coconut
aminos, soy sauce, liquid
aminos, or mirin

⅓ cup [115 g] honey, ⅓ cup
[115 g] maple syrup,
or ⅓ cup [65 g] brown
sugar

FOR THE STUFFING

2 sweet peppers,
seeded and thinly sliced

1 onion, thinly sliced

2 to 4 garlic cloves,
finely chopped

Handful of fresh parsley
or other fresh herbs,
finely chopped

1 lemon, sliced

Generous drizzle of olive oil

Flaky sea salt

Generous splash of white
wine

FOR THE FISH

1 whole fish (flathead,
salmon, trout, or similar),
gutted and scaled

Flaky sea salt and freshly
ground black pepper

BEFORE YOU HEAD OUT

To make the marinade ahead of time (if using):
In a food processor or blender, combine the
hot peppers, shallots, garlic, ginger, coconut
aminos, and honey until smooth. Store in
a tightly sealed mason jar in your cooler. If
preparing at camp, use a pestle and mortar to
mash it all together as best you can, or, if you
haven't brought one, a bowl with the back of
a spoon works too.

NOTE: If you opt not to use
a marinade, you can simply
rub the fish with olive oil,
garlic, and salt after stuffing.

AT THE CAMPSITE

Build a big fire and let it burn down to a
medium flame with a consistent bed of coals.

To make the stuffing:
Combine the sweet peppers, onion, garlic,
herbs, lemon, olive oil, sea salt, and white wine
in a bowl, tossing to coat. Set aside and allow
the flavors to familiarize for at least 5 minutes.

To make the fish:
Make sure the fish is clean and check if the
opening is large enough for your stuffing. If
it's too small, carefully cut along the inside of
the fish, working toward the backbone to create
more space. Pack in your stuffing mixture,
packing tight but not too full. Depending on
the size of your fish, take one or two large
sheets of aluminum foil and lay them out, over-
lapping by at least 3 in [7.5 cm]. Put the fish on

◄◄ CONTINUED ►►

top, and, if using the marinade, spoon it generously over the entire fish. Be sure to seal up the foil packet nice and tight.

Take note of how big your fish is, scaling your cooking time accordingly. Place the packet on a grill grate over coals and cook for about 1 hour for a large fish or 20 to 40 minutes for a smaller one. Be mindful to feed your fire and maintain your bed of coals. Flip and cook for another 20 minutes to 1 hour, making sure the meat is cooked through and the eyes have gone opaque.

To serve, dig in family-style or separate portions for tacos or salad—look out for bones and enjoy while hot.

GIANT SNICKERDOODLE S'MORES

SERVES 4 TO 8
Medium heat; open flame

Nothing says camping quite like s'mores! While there are endless variations on this camping classic, our favorite starts at home with snickerdoodle cookies. We use the pan-banging method during baking to achieve thin, toothsome cookies to replace the traditional graham crackers. Milk chocolate is swapped out for hazelnut chocolate spread, creating a gooey cookie sandwich that's big on texture and flavor. We opt for big cookies and two marshmallows on each sandwich, but smaller ones are equally delicious. Bake the cookies well ahead of your camping trip; they'll stay fresh for a week or two.

◄◄ CONTINUED ►►

FOR THE SNICKERDOODLES

1 cup [220 g] unsalted butter, at room temperature

1 cup [200 g] granulated sugar, plus 1 Tbsp for coating cookie dough balls

¾ cup [150 g] light brown sugar

2 cups [280 g] all-purpose flour

1 tsp chai spice, freshly ground nutmeg, or allspice

1 tsp baking soda

½ tsp cream of tartar

½ tsp kosher salt

1 large egg

1 tsp vanilla extract

1 tsp cinnamon

FOR THE S'MORES

2 large marshmallows per s'more

Chocolate hazelnut spread, such as Nutella

To make the snickerdoodles ahead of time: Preheat the oven to 350°F [180°C]. Line a baking sheet with parchment paper.

In the bowl of a stand mixer, cream together the butter and sugars until light and fluffy, about 5 minutes.

In another bowl, whisk together the flour, baking soda, cream of tartar, and salt.

Add the egg and vanilla to the butter and sugar mixture on low speed until just combined. Slowly add the flour mixture on low speed until uniform, being careful not to overmix.

Sprinkle the cinnamon and remaining 1 Tbsp of granulated sugar onto a plate or shallow bowl and stir to combine. Using your hands, roll the dough into doughnut hole–size balls, then roll each gently in the cinnamon-sugar mixture to coat. Place each cookie dough ball 3 in [7.5 cm] apart on the prepared baking sheet (the cookies will spread significantly—we usually bake six cookies at a time).

Bake for a total of 11 to 13 minutes, but intermittently bang the sheet to help the cookies flatten. For example: Set the timer for 5 minutes, then remove the sheet and drop it from about 12 in [30 cm] onto the counter. Set the timer for another 5 minutes and repeat. Finish baking for another minute or two until the edges are crisp but not browned, remove from the oven, and allow to cool on the sheet completely before stashing them away in an airtight container.

AT THE CAMPSITE

To make the s'mores:

Roast one or two marshmallows over the fire to your preferred doneness—we recommend a good charred exterior with a molten interior. Slather two snickerdoodle cookies with chocolate hazelnut spread and sandwich the roasted marshmallows between.

TAKE IT FURTHER

Experiment with your favorite cookies, crisps, crackers, and spreads to make your very own signature s'mores recipe. Some of our favorite modifications include using caramel-filled chocolate bars, peanut butter, or even toasted sourdough bread!

CAMPFIRE BERRY CRUMBLE

SERVES 4
Medium heat; low flame or hot coals

A good skillet cobbler is a summertime staple. Quick and effortless, this crowd-pleasing one-dish dessert is easy to adapt; use any regional berries or stone fruits in their peak season. We make ours with peaches, blueberries, and marionberries, which are a cultivated hybrid of wild blackberry varietals, bountifully available during summer in the Pacific Northwest. Floral, tangy peaches play off the sugary-sweetness and acidity of the berries, all cooking down into a delightfully jammy texture underneath a soft, crumbly top. Tahini brings a new layer of toasty, nutty flavor to the classic crumble topping. The aroma rising slowly as it all cooks and bubbles over hot coals can conjure up an appetite even after a very filling meal. Swap peaches for nectarines or plums, and harvest wild blueberries, blackberries, and raspberries if you can.

GATHER

½ cup [110 g] salted butter,
at ambient temperature,
plus more for greasing the
skillet

1 heaping Tbsp tahini

½ tsp almond or vanilla
extract

¼ cup [50 g] granulated
sugar

¼ cup [50 g] light brown
sugar

1 cup [140 g] all-purpose
flour

1 cup [100 g] rolled oats

½ tsp cinnamon

Pinch of flaky sea salt

FOR THE BERRIES

1½ cups [210 g] fresh, wild,
or frozen blueberries

1 cup [120 g] marionberries
or blackberries

1 large, ripe peach or
2 smaller ones, pitted
and sliced

BEFORE YOU HEAD OUT

To make the crumble topping ahead of time:
Combine the butter, tahini, almond extract,
and sugars in a large mixing bowl until uniform.
Add the flour and oats gradually, sprinkling
in the cinnamon and a pinch of flaky sea salt.
Break up big clumps but allow the texture to
have some variation. The consistency of the
crumble dough should be dry but malleable.

AT THE CAMPSITE

To make the berries:
Add the berries and sliced peaches directly to
a large or medium buttered sauté pan or skillet,
creating an even layer of mixed fruit. Crumble
on the topping, lightly pressing down so it holds
its shape. If your skillet doesn't have a lid, cover
with aluminum foil, securing it around the sides,
or with another larger cast-iron pan. Cook over
a low flame or hot coals, rotating the pan to
maintain an even distribution of heat. Cook
for 10 to 20 minutes, depending on the heat, or
until the fruit nectar is bubbling and the crumble topping has some crispiness. Remove from
the heat, allow to cool for a moment, and enjoy
warm, maybe even right out of the skillet.

TAKE IT FURTHER

*Add a dollop of fresh Mason Jar Whipped Cream
(page 121), crème fraîche, or vanilla ice cream if
you've got it!*

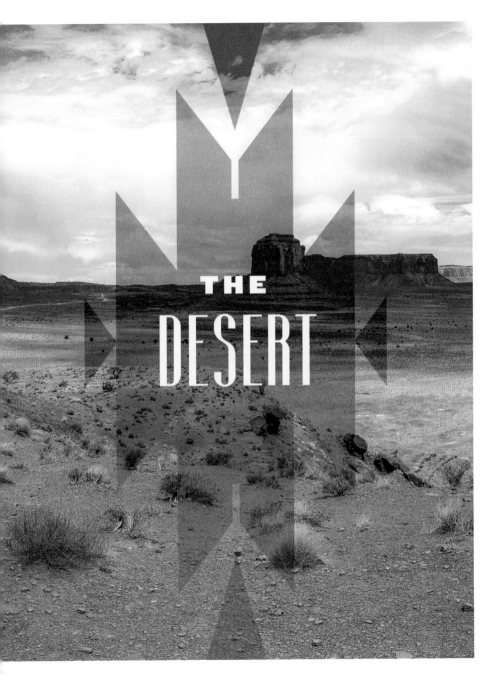

THE
DESERT

PRAIRIE BREAKFAST BURRITO

SERVES 1 OR 2
Medium heat; coals

When you need something to keep you going all morning, breakfast burritos are here to serve. Filling, customizable, and real crowd-pleasers, they're one of our absolute go-to recipes no matter the region. Consider this something you can easily modify based on what you have on hand and what you're in the mood for. It's plenty forgiving, and we promise you'll get really good at wrapping burritos in no time. This is a recipe for one big burrito, which can easily be cut in half to serve two campers.

GATHER

FOR A MEAT BURRITO

1 chorizo sausage

FOR A VEGGIE BURRITO

Ghee or butter

2 handfuls of diced
mushrooms, onions, and
bell pepper

2 eggs

Handful of grated
Monterey Jack or Cheddar
cheese

1 flour tortilla

1 avocado, sliced

Salsa or hot sauce

Fresh cilantro (optional)

BEFORE YOU HEAD OUT

Feel free to grate your cheeses ahead of time,
measuring out the needed quantities and storing
in an airtight container. Freshly grated cheese
is best, but prepping a day ahead will save time
fireside and won't compromise flavor.

AT THE CAMPSITE

Start a fire and let it burn down until you have
a nice bed of coals to cook over. We like to use
one skillet for this, but you can use two and
cook straight on the coals or over a grill grate.

To make a meat burrito:
Add your chorizo to the pan, using a spatula,
spoon, or fork to smash it up and cook it through.
Once cooked, push the chorizo to the side of
the pan and add the eggs. Scramble them up
and, just before they're finished, add a handful
of cheese and mix in the chorizo.

To make a veggie burrito:
Add a little ghee or butter to the pan and sauté
the mushrooms, onions, and bell peppers. Once
cooked and slightly browned, push them to the
side of the pan and add the eggs. Scramble them
up and, just before the eggs are finished, add a
handful of cheese and mix in the veggies.

◄◄ CONTINUED ►►

To assemble:

Lightly warm the tortilla over the fire, in your other skillet, or straight on the grill grate so it's easier to work with. Next, scoop the egg mixture into the middle of the tortilla, adding slices of fresh avocado, salsa, and cilantro as you like.

To wrap, fold up the bottom edge, then one side, then the top, then roll the open side closed.

TAKE IT FURTHER

Make it a real cowboy burrito and grill it! Wipe out your skillet and quickly grill your burrito on both sides so it's nice and warm and slightly charred on the outside. Slather with salsa on a plate and dig in.

HONEY STUFFED FRENCH TOAST

SERVES 4
Medium-low heat; low coals

One common misconception is that camping is not luxurious, and we think that couldn't be further from the truth. Waking up refreshed, easing into the day, and soaking in the scenery is only made sweeter with Honey Stuffed French Toast worthy of an upscale cafe. On top of that, French toast is the best way we know to give new life to day-old bread. We prefer a thick, country-style loaf like sourdough, but you can really use any bread—just keep in mind that it's soaking up a custard mix, so if it's soft and thin, you're going to have softer French toast. Remember: Whisk, dunk, cook, top, serve. It really is that simple and—you guessed it—delicious.

◀◀ CONTINUED ▶▶

GATHER

1 cup [240 g] whole-milk ricotta cheese

3 to 4 Tbsp honey, plus more for serving (optional)

Pinch of kosher salt

Pinch of freshly ground black pepper

Zest and juice of 1 small orange (optional)

FOR THE TOAST

4 or 5 eggs, depending on how much your bread soaks up

¼ cup [60 ml] whole milk, buttermilk, or half-and-half

1 to 2 tsp vanilla extract

1 tsp cinnamon

8 slices thick bread, such as sourdough or country loaf

1 to 2 Tbsp butter

BEFORE YOU HEAD OUT

To make the Honey Whipped Ricotta ahead of time:
Place the ricotta, honey, salt, pepper, and orange juice (if using) in a food processor and blend until smooth. It should take about 1 minute. Fold in the orange zest (if using). Store in an airtight container or mason jar in your cooler.

AT THE CAMPSITE

Build a fire and let it burn down to very low coals. If you're cooking other things at the same time that need a higher heat, place your sauté pan or skillet off to the side of the fire so you maintain a nice even, low heat.

To make the toast:
In a bowl, shallow pan, or resealable container, whisk together the eggs, milk, vanilla, and cinnamon. Dredge each slice of bread in the mix by dunking one side and then the other so that they're all fully coated. Depending on your method, you can either dunk all the bread at once, setting the slices aside until you're ready to cook, or you can prepare a slice or two at a time, or however many your pan can hold.

In your pan, melt a little butter and add as many slices of bread as you can. Cook for 3 to

5 minutes, checking to make sure it doesn't burn. Once golden brown and a little toasty, flip and cook for another 3 minutes, or until browned. Continue until you've cooked up all the slices.

To serve, place one slice of bread on each plate. Add a dollop of whipped ricotta, top with another slice of bread, and finish with either more ricotta or a drizzle of honey. Serve warm and, ideally, with a cup of coffee.

TAKE IT FURTHER

Mix it up with the ricotta! You can enhance your ricotta by adding fresh berries, herbs, or anything else that sounds good. You can also keep it simple and just use maple syrup. If you want to kick it up a notch, try warming your maple syrup with a dram of whiskey and a few cinnamon sticks. If you've got extra spices on hand, try adding cardamom or something similar to your custard.

CHILAQUILES WITH CRUMBLY CHEESE

Chilaquiles is a traditional Mexican breakfast dish created to give new life to yesterday's tortillas. Essentially tortilla chips smothered in salsa, this dish has endless variations, all equally delicious in their own right. Our recipe is created for simplicity and speed with a cast-iron skillet, making it a perfect solution for larger groups. We use store-bought corn tortilla chips, but making your own from tortillas works great— whether cut into triangles and set out overnight to become stale, or quickly flash-fried in a shallow bath of vegetable oil. Tomatillos are an essential ingredient; they are in season summer through fall and often available at farmers' markets. Roast your tomatillos and jalapeños at home before packing the cooler to achieve the charred, smoky flavors needed.

GATHER

8 medium tomatillos or several smaller ones, husked and rinsed

2 jalapeño peppers, stemmed and seeded

2 Tbsp high-heat oil, such as safflower or grapeseed

1 small onion, diced

Flaky sea salt and freshly ground pepper

3 garlic cloves, finely chopped

Big pinch of red pepper flakes

1 cup [240 ml] vegetable or chicken broth

1 small bag or ½ large bag of corn tortilla chips

Handful of fresh cilantro, chopped

6 oz [170 g] crumbly cheese, such as feta or cotija

BEFORE YOU HEAD OUT

Heat your broiler and put the whole tomatillos and prepped jalapeños on a baking sheet. Broil until the tomatillos appear charred, 3 to 5 minutes, and then flip them over to continue roasting. Being careful not to over-char, remove from the oven after another 3 to 5 minutes. Allow to cool and store in an airtight container.

AT THE CAMPSITE

Heat the oil in a large sauté pan or skillet over medium heat and add the onions, seasoning with salt and pepper. While they begin to soften and become fragrant, dice the roasted tomatillos and jalapeños and stir them in. Cook for 3 to 5 minutes until everything is nicely incorporated, and add the garlic and red pepper flakes, continuing to stir. As the mixture softens and begins to brown, pour in the broth and allow to simmer for about 10 minutes.

◄◄ CONTINUED ►►

Remove the pan from the heat and gently stir in the tortilla chips, making sure to evenly coat with the tomatillo salsa mixture, allowing the chips to soften in the sauce.

To serve, either pile plates or bowls high with chilaquiles, or enjoy straight out of the skillet, topped with freshly chopped cilantro, lots of crumbled cheese, salt, pepper, and red pepper flakes.

TAKE IT FURTHER

Fry one sunny-side-up egg per camper in a smaller skillet on the side, placing each on top of a heaping plate of chilaquiles before topping with the cilantro and cheese.

SKILLET FLATBREADS

SERVES 4
Medium heat; stove or flame

This versatile campfire bread is perfect for sopping up stews and soups or even swapping in place of store-bought buns and tortillas. The one-to-one ingredient ratios make it easy to double or halve the recipe for bigger or smaller groups. We love to experiment with different spices and herbs added into the dough, playing off the flavors of whatever else we're cooking up.

◄◄ CONTINUED ►►

GATHER

1 cup [140 g] all-purpose or whole-wheat flour

1 cup [240 g] Greek yogurt

Splash of olive oil

1 tsp flaky sea salt

FOR GARLICKY FLATBREAD

2 garlic cloves, finely chopped

1 tsp fresh or dried oregano or rosemary, chopped

1 tsp onion powder

Handful of chopped fresh parsley

FOR LEMON-HERB FLATBREAD

Zest of 1 lemon, plus a squeeze of juice

Handful of chopped fresh herbs, such as sage, dill, mint, sorrel, or rosemary

½ cup [120 g] ricotta cheese (optional, to replace half the yogurt of the base recipe)

FOR CURRY-SPICED FLATBREAD

1 Tbsp sesame seeds

1 tsp cumin seed, ground or whole

1 tsp coriander seed, ground or whole

Flaky sea salt and freshly ground black pepper

Dash of turmeric powder

Dash of paprika

AT THE CAMPSITE

In a mixing bowl, combine the flour with the yogurt, olive oil, and salt, adding a splash of water here and there until the dough is uniform. It should be dry but not crumbly. If the dough becomes too sticky, sprinkle in some more flour. Fold in the desired spices, herbs, and seasonings. Let the dough rest.

Bring a glug of olive oil to medium heat in a large cast-iron sauté pan or skillet over hot coals or a low flame. With floured hands, pinch off a meatball-size dough ball and flatten between your palms, stretching and forming it into a flat, uniform circle, a ½ in [12 mm] thick or thinner. Throw the dough round directly onto the skillet, cooking until browned around the edges. Flip and cook on the other side until some char starts to appear. Repeat with the remaining dough.

Serve hot out of the skillet with our White Bean Chili (page 113) or Simple Mushroom Shakshuka (page 46), or make it into a sandwich.

Alternate cooking method:
Using a grill grate over a low or medium flame, oil and cook your flatbread dough rounds directly on the grate. Use tongs to flip. This cooking method will yield a more flame-charred, crispier bread with a smokier flavor.

PUMPKIN SAGE POLENTA

SERVES 4
Medium heat; stove

This dish is especially satisfying in cooler weather thanks to the comforting warmth of pumpkin and sage. The trick to making creamy polenta is to never stop stirring. Since it's so important to get the heat right on this recipe, we recommend using a gas camp stove instead of a fire, but if you're comfortable controlling heat, the smoky flavor of the open flame is a great addition. If you don't have pumpkin, you could swap in any other vegetable puree at a one-to-one ratio, but we'd recommend sticking to roots, gourds, or cauliflower over greens.

GATHER

3 Tbsp ghee or salted butter

2 shallots, minced

2 garlic cloves, minced

4 cups [960 ml] vegetable broth, low sodium if you can

1 cup [140 g] polenta

1 cup [256 g] canned pumpkin

1 tsp flaky sea salt

1 tsp freshly ground black pepper

½ tsp paprika

¼ tsp dried thyme

¼ tsp dried sage

Fresh herbs and grated cheese, for garnishing (optional)

AT THE CAMPSITE

In a sauté pan over low heat, add the ghee, shallots, and garlic, sweating for about 2 minutes—be careful not to burn the garlic. Turn the heat up to medium and add the vegetable broth, gently simmering. Begin to add the polenta, ¼ to ⅓ cup [35 to 45 g] at a time, stirring constantly. Once you've added all the polenta, drop the heat back down to low and cook for 20 to 25 minutes, stirring frequently, until the polenta has absorbed all the liquid and is soft.

Add the pumpkin and spices, stirring to incorporate. Let cook for a few more minutes and then grab your bowls to plate it up. We like to garnish with fresh herbs and cheese.

TAKE IT FURTHER

Top that delicious bowl of pumpkin polenta with balsamic roasted veggies—baby broccoli, onions, beets, celeriac, or anything that sounds tasty. Sage leaves fried in butter are another good topping and they're just as easy as they sound. Heat some butter in a pan over high heat until it's crackling, toss in whole sage leaves, add a little salt, and stir until crisp. Allow to cool slightly before sprinkling over the polenta.

CAMPFIRE GRILLED PIZZA

MAKES 1 PIZZA
Medium-high heat; hot coals

A crowd-pleaser for sure, pizza is beloved for its simplicity and adaptability. It's a great way to connect with friends, use up ingredients, feed a crowd, and maybe even have breakfast sorted for the morning. We prefer to use sourdough pizza dough, but whatever you can get (or make) works fine—just make sure you've got plenty of tasty toppings to do the heavy lifting.

GATHER

One 1 lb [450 g] store-bought pizza dough ball

One 12 oz [340 g] can marinara sauce

1 cup [120 g] grated mozzarella cheese

¾ cup [180 g] ricotta

2 Tbsp grated Parmesan cheese

2 garlic cloves, minced (optional)

Your choice of toppings

BEFORE YOU HEAD OUT

Buy some premade pizza dough from your local shop—get sourdough, if you can—or grab one from the refrigerated section at the grocery store. Rather than bringing a bunch of flour, you can put just a little in a jar so you have enough to flour your cutting board and hands. If you've never made pizza before, practice beforehand so you'll be an expert when you get to camp.

AT THE CAMPSITE

Make a fire and let it burn down to medium-high heat so you can spread out the coals and set up your grill grate.

The first thing is to parcook (which just means half-bake) the pizza crust. To start, grab a cutting board and lightly flour the surface and your hands. Next, turn out the dough and begin to shape it into a pizza round; the size depends on how thick you want it.

Next, lightly oil the grill grate and then put the dough right on top, letting it cook on one side for a few minutes and then flipping to the other. You'll know it's time to flip when you see a little color developing on the bottom and bubbles forming on the top. It'll be hot, so be sure to use your tongs to flip. Pull the

◄◄ CONTINUED ►►

parcooked pizza crust from the fire and put it on the cutting board for assembly.

Spoon a little marinara onto the center, using the back of your spoon to spread it all the way out to the edge, leaving ¼ to ½ in [6 to 12 mm] for your crust. Next, add the cheeses, completely covering the marinara and spreading evenly. We like to add a little fresh garlic on top here, but that's up to you. Top with whatever you'd like—sausage and peppers, grilled onions and roasted corn, cherry tomatoes and mushrooms, prosciutto and olives—and finish back on the fire to melt the cheese, 3 to 5 minutes. Pull from the fire, cut into slices, and enjoy.

TAKE IT FURTHER

Try adding fresh herbs, such as basil, mint, or rosemary, to the pizza after grilling. A drizzle of balsamic reduction goes a long way. Try a white pizza, swapping the marinara for garlic and lemon. The possibilities are endless, and you'll surely invent your favorite combination of toppings.

WHITE BEAN CHILI

SERVES 4
Medium heat; flame or hot coals

On a cold night in the desert, there's nothing quite like a hot bowl of hearty bean chili. Our take on this classic combines the warming flavors of ginger and red pepper with creamy stewed white beans and potatoes. Nutrient-dense greens and a big dollop of lemony yogurt round out the meal. Try a side of our Skillet Flatbreads (page 105) to sop up every last drop and morsel.

◀◀ CONTINUED ▶▶

GATHER

¼ cup [60 ml] olive oil, plus more for drizzling

1 small or ½ large onion, diced

1 carrot, diced

1 Tbsp butter

3 garlic cloves, finely chopped

2 in [5 cm] piece ginger, diced or grated

Flaky sea salt and freshly ground pepper

Red pepper flakes

1 large or a handful of small potatoes, chopped

1 cup [160 g] white beans, such as cannellini or butter beans, either dried and presoaked or canned

4 cups [960 ml] vegetable broth or chicken stock

Zest and juice of 1 lemon

2 handfuls of hearty dark greens, such as kale or Swiss chard, deribbed

Greek yogurt, for serving

BEFORE YOU HEAD OUT

Dried beans are magic: Not only are they economical and shelf-stable, but oftentimes the rarest and most flavorful varieties are available only in their dried state. Soaked and drained beans will keep in the cooler for days—presoak and store your beans according to their instructions, or soak on-site ahead of time. Canned beans work perfectly well, just make sure you pack a can opener and a small strainer for rinsing.

AT THE CAMPSITE

In your deepest sauté pan, skillet, pot, or Dutch oven, heat the olive oil over medium heat, then add the onion and carrot. Add a dab of butter for good measure. When the onion begins to soften, add the garlic and ginger and stir. Season with salt, pepper, and red pepper flakes. When those become aromatic, about 1 minute, add the potatoes. If your onions start browning too quickly, deglaze with a splash of water, beer, or white wine. Add the beans and season again with salt, pepper, and red pepper flakes. Continue to cook, stirring occasionally, until the beans and potatoes start to brown, about 5 minutes, using a wooden spoon to smash some of the beans against the side of the pot or skillet. This helps create a thick, creamy texture.

Next, add the stock and 1 tsp of the lemon juice. Simmer until the chili reduces to a thick consistency, stirring in the chopped greens right before removing from the heat, allowing them a moment to wilt and soften in the chili.

Serve hot in deep bowls with a big dollop of yogurt, fresh lemon zest and the remaining juice, salt and pepper, and a drizzle of olive oil.

TAKE IT FURTHER

Try adding in a few slices of chopped bacon while browning your onions for a heartier, protein-heavy stew. If you and your campmates prefer a spicier meal, try seasoning with chili powder throughout the cooking process or add your favorite hot sauce before digging in.

BRATWURST SANDWICHES WITH BEER ONIONS AND KRAUT

SERVES 4 TO 6
Medium heat; open flame

Bratwurst is a delicious camp cuisine however you prepare it. Whether roasted on a stick over an open flame or sautéed with beer and onions, served on a platter with sides of mustard and sauerkraut or covered in cheese on a crusty bun, this fatty German sausage makes an excellent main course for very hungry campers. Our favorite way to prepare and serve bratwurst combines every delicious version into one handheld sandwich, easily assembled to order. While any type of brat-wurst will do, keep an eye out at the grocery store for Käse Krainer, an Austrian bratwurst filled with Swiss cheese.

GATHER

2 Tbsp salted butter

1 yellow onion, thinly sliced

Flaky sea salt and freshly ground pepper

One 12 oz [360 ml] can session German or American beer, such as a pilsner, lager, or pale ale

4 to 6 links bratwurst, at ambient temperature

4 to 6 hot dog buns, rolls, or pretzel buns

4 Tbsp [60 g] mayonnaise

4 Tbsp [60 g] grainy mustard

8 oz [230 g] sauerkraut

4 oz [115 g] Swiss, Gruyère, or Emmentaler cheese

AT THE CAMPSITE

First, decide whether you want to cook your brats in the skillet or roast them over the open flame. If you're roasting, find and prepare a good skewer stick for each camper.

In a large sauté pan or skillet over medium heat, melt half of the butter and add the onions, stirring to coat. Season with salt and pepper. Allow the onions to soften, but remove from the heat if they're in danger of becoming crispy. When the onions become translucent, splash in about a quarter of the beer and stir, allowing the beer to cook off while the onions continue to soften and brown, another 5 to 10 minutes. Remove your bratwurst links from the packaging and score the casing with a sharp knife.

To make the brats in the skillet:
Remove the onions and keep the pan hot. Melt the rest of the butter and add your bratwurst, sizzling to cook and brown, 3 to 5 minutes. Add a splash of beer, flip, and cook on the other side for another 3 to 5 minutes. Push the brats to the side.

Slather the buns with mayonnaise, toasting them mayonnaise-side down in the hot pan until golden brown. Remove the pan from the heat for assembly.

◄◄ CONTINUED ►►

To roast the brats:

Push the onions to the cooler side of the pan over low heat. Skewer each brat securely and roast over the open flame, rotating to cook and char evenly.

Meanwhile, slather the inside of the buns with mayonnaise and toast them in the pan, mayonnaise-side down, until golden brown. Remove the pan from the heat for assembly.

To assemble the sandwiches:

With a toasted bun in hand, slather each side with mustard. Add beer-cooked onions and sauerkraut, then the charred bratwurst, topped with a slice of cheese—the heat of the bratwurst will warm and melt the cheese just enough. Top with more kraut and onions, if desired, and enjoy hot.

WHISKEY BANANAS

SERVES 4
Medium heat; stove, low flame, or hot coals

Quick, rich, and layered with a depth of flavor you can only really get with smoke and liquor, these bananas make for the perfect nightcap dessert any time of year. If you're craving something sweet for breakfast, they're a perfect addition to a stack of pancakes too. We like to use just-ripe bananas (without any brown spots) so they keep their shape, but you can really use whatever you've got. Feel free to toss in a handful of blueberries or any other spare fruits. The mix of smoke and sweet fruit is undercut nicely with freshly whipped cream that anyone can help make. That being said, if you're making these bananas with kids, leave the whiskey out and add a dash of vanilla extract instead.

◄◄ CONTINUED ►►

GATHER

½ cup [110 g] salted butter

½ cup [100 g] packed brown sugar

½ cup [120 ml] whiskey

4 large bananas, peeled and halved lengthwise

1 recipe Mason Jar Whipped Cream (page 121)

AT THE CAMPSITE

In a cast-iron sauté pan or skillet over medium heat, melt the butter and stir in the brown sugar. Next, carefully add the whiskey. Heat to a low boil, stirring gently so the sugar dissolves and nothing begins to stick. Add the bananas to the pan and simmer, spooning the syrup over the bananas until they're tender and shiny with glaze. Be careful not to overcook so they don't get mushy. (However, if they do, don't worry! Just smash them all together and serve in a bowl, with chopped nuts for texture.) Remove from the heat and allow to cool slightly before serving.

Scoop into a bowl, top with the whipped cream, and enjoy.

MASON JAR WHIPPED CREAM

MAKES 1 PT [480 ML]
No heat

We make this simple whipped cream whenever there's an excuse, and there's almost always an excuse. Since it doesn't require any heat, just a little effort, this a great recipe to recruit the kids for. The more you make it, the more you'll start to play around with flavors, spiking it with spices just to see what happens. Be sure to pack a 1 pt [480 ml] mason jar and have it at ambient temperature and at the ready for this recipe.

◄◄ CONTINUED ►►

GATHER

1 cup [240 ml] cold heavy whipping cream

½ tsp vanilla extract (optional)

Pinch of granulated sugar

Dash of cinnamon

AT THE CAMPSITE

Fill the mason jar halfway with cold whipping cream, add the vanilla (if using), sugar, and cinnamon, and secure the lid. Begin shaking. You'll know it's ready when you don't hear the cream swooshing around anymore and the sides of your jar are coated in airy, fluffy cream. If you shake too much, the solids will separate and you'll end up with a sweet spiced butter for pancakes in the morning. Add the whipped cream to Campfire Berry Crumble (page 92), Whiskey Bananas (page 119), or Blackberry and Herb Pancakes (page 36), and savor by the fire.

TAKE IT FURTHER

Depending on how vigorously you shake, this method takes anywhere from 1 to 3 minutes and it's easily modified when it comes to spices and flavorings. We use vanilla and cinnamon, but other flavors, such as garam masala, nutmeg, or bourbon, work great too—just use similar quantities to what's listed above.

PENDLETON CAMPFIRE POPCORN

SERVES 4

Medium heat; low flame or hot coals

Fireside popcorn is a treat we can't help but indulge in. Handfuls of fluffy, fresh popped corn with your favorite seasonings will be a go-to crowd-pleaser on many trips. Experiment with flavors and seasonings that fit the mood: miso honey butter for a salty-sweet snack, ranch flavor for something more savory, or Parmesan and herbs for something a little fancier.

◄◄ CONTINUED ►►

GATHER

1 glug high-heat oil, such as safflower, avocado, or canola

½ cup [100 g] popcorn kernels

3 Tbsp salted butter

FOR HIGH DESERT RANCH SEASONING (MAKES ABOUT ¾ CUP [70 G])

½ cup [63 g] powdered buttermilk

¼ cup [5 g] nutritional yeast

1 Tbsp onion powder

1 tsp dried chives

1 tsp dried sage

1 tsp dried rosemary

½ tsp dried thyme

½ tsp dried dill

½ tsp garlic powder

Flaky sea salt (optional)

FOR MISO HONEY SEASONING

1 tsp white miso paste

1 tsp honey

Flaky sea salt

FOR HERBED PARMESAN SEASONING

3 oz [85 g] Parmesan cheese, grated

1 to 2 tsp herbs, fresh or dried, such as rosemary, sage, or thyme

Drizzle of olive oil

Flaky sea salt and freshly ground black pepper

BEFORE YOU HEAD OUT

We like to make a big batch of high desert ranch seasoning to keep stocked in the pantry for popcorn, home fries, potato salads, and more.

To make the high desert ranch seasoning:

Whisk together all the ingredients until uniform and store in an airtight jar. You can find most of these ingredients in the baking and spice sections, or dehydrate your own herbs on a baking sheet with a silicone mat in the oven at 175°F [80°C] for 20 to 30 minutes, or until the herbs are completely dry and break at the touch. Kept in a cool, dry place, this batch of dry seasoning will stay fresh for months.

AT THE CAMPSITE

Heat the oil and popcorn kernels in a lidded pot over a medium flame or raised over hot coals. As kernels begin to pop, shake the pot over the heat, almost continuously, to keep anything from sticking or burning. Listen to the kernels popping and remove from the heat when you can count 4 full seconds in between pops. Pour the popcorn into a large bowl or into campers' individual bowls.

In the hot pot, melt the butter until foamy and drizzle over the popcorn, tossing to coat.

To make the high desert ranch popcorn:

Sprinkle 1 to 2 Tbsp of your homemade ranch seasoning over hot, buttery popcorn, tossing to evenly coat. Add salt (if desired) and experiment with the addition of other fresh herbs and oils for flavor.

◄◄ CONTINUED ►►

To make the miso honey popcorn:
Add the white miso paste directly to the pot with the melted butter, stirring or whisking vigorously to combine. Pour the miso butter mixture over the popcorn, and drizzle honey from a spoon, tossing to coat evenly. Sprinkle with flaky sea salt.

To make the herbed parmesan popcorn:
Grate about 2 Tbsp of the Parmesan into the melting butter in the hot pot and stir or whisk vigorously to melt and combine. Drizzle the cheesy butter mixture over the hot popcorn, tossing to distribute. Sprinkle in the herbs and grate ample Parmesan over the popcorn, mixing as you go. Add a drizzle of olive oil, a sprinkle of flaky sea salt, and a few good turns of freshly ground black pepper.